Curious **Kids** Guides

DINOSAURS

Rod Theodorou

KINGFISHER
NEW YORK

KINGFISHER
LONDON & NEW YORK

Copyright © 1994 by Kingfisher
Published in the United States by Kingfisher,
175 Fifth Ave., New York, NY 10010
Kingfisher is an imprint of Macmillan Children's Books, London.
All rights reserved.
Distributed in the U.S. by Macmillan, 175 Fifth Ave., New York, NY 10010
Distributed in Canada by H.B. Fenn and Company Ltd.,
34 Nixon Road, Bolton, Ontario L7E 1W2
LIBRARY OF CONGRESS CATALOGING-IN-PUBLICATION DATA
Theodorou, Rod.
    Dinosaurs / by Rod Theodorou.
    p. cm.—(Curious kids guides)
    Summary: A variety of information on dinosaurs is presented in
question and answer format.
    ISBN-13: 978-0-7534-5474-9
    ISBN-10: 0-7534-5474-2
    1. Dinosaurs—Miscellanea—Juvenile literature. [1. Dinosaurs—
Miscellanea. 2. Questions and answers.] I. Title. II. Series.
QE861.5 .T47 2002
567.9—dc21
2002069537
ISBN: 978-0-7534-5474-9

Kingfisher books are available for special promotions and premiums.
For details contact: Special Markets Department,
Macmillan, 175 Fifth Avenue, New York, NY 10010.
For more information, please visit www.kingfisherpublications.com
Printed in Taiwan
9 8 7 6 5 4 3
3TR/0110/SHEN/UD UNV/126.6MA

Series editor: Jackie Gaff
Series designer: David West Children's Books
Author: Rod Theodorou
Consultant: Dougal Dixon
Editor: Brigid Avison
Art editor: Christina Fraser
Illustrations (including cover): Chris Forsey;
    Tony Kenyon (B L Kearley) all cartoons.

CONTENTS

How many dinosaurs were there?

There were lots of different dinosaurs. Scientists have already named about 300 kinds, and new ones are being found all the time. Some dinosaurs were big, others were tiny. Some were fierce meat-eaters, others were gentle vegetarians that browsed on plants.

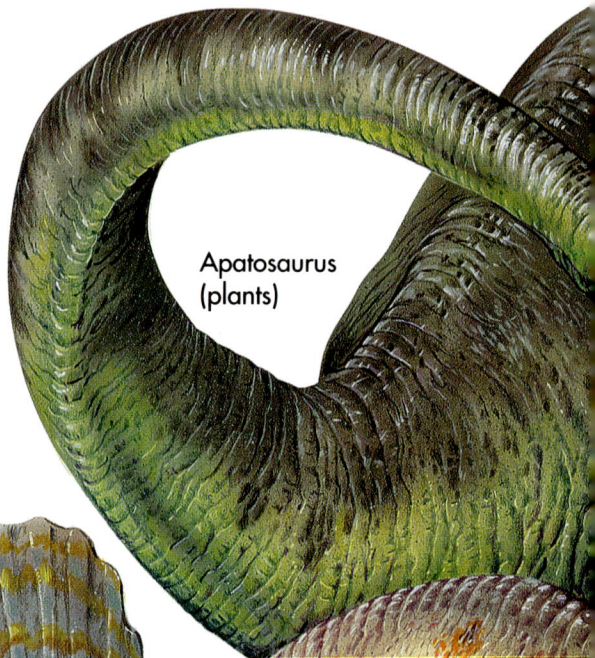

Apatosaurus (plants)

Spinosaurus (meat)

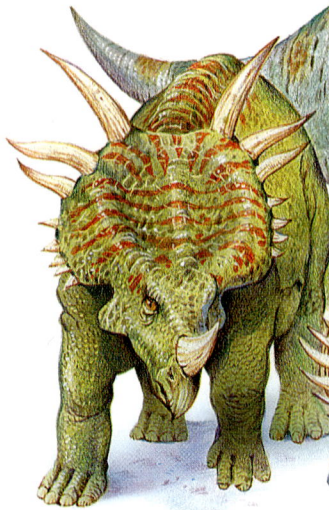

Iguanodon (plants)

Styracosaurus (plants)   Panoplosaurus (plants)   Oviraptor (meat)   Stygimoloch (plants)

• Dinosaurs were reptiles. Today's reptiles include lizards, crocodiles, tortoises, and snakes.

• Like most other reptiles, dinosaurs lived on land and had dry, scaly skin. Their eggs had leathery shells, unlike birds' eggs which are hard and brittle.

How long ago did dinosaurs live?

Dinosaurs lived MILLIONS and MILLIONS of years ago. The first ones appeared about 230 million years ago, and the last ones we know about died out over 65 million years ago. Compared to this, human history is just a hiccup — we've only been around for the last 2 million years.

• Dinosaurs ruled the Earth for a mind-boggling 165 million years!

Kentrosaurus (plants)

Why was Tyrannosaurus a big mouth?

Tyrannosaurus was a huge meat-eater. At about 20 feet (6 m) high, it stood three times taller than a grizzly bear. Its mouth was huge, too — big enough to swallow you whole!

● Many people think Tyrannosaurus could have run as fast as 30 miles an hour (50 km/h) when chasing a meal!

● This is how big one of Tyrannosaurus's teeth was. The rough edges helped to rip through skin and flesh.

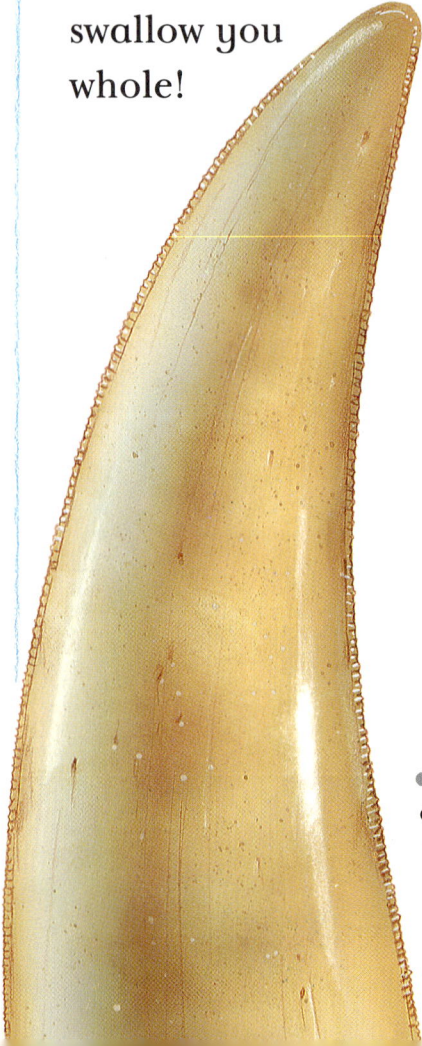

- The name Tyrannosaurus means "tyrant lizard" — a tyrant is a cruel king.

Was Tyrannosaurus king of the dinosaurs?

There may have been even bigger meat-eaters than Tyrannosaurus. The tall dinosaur on the right is Deinocheirus. We have to guess what it looked like, as we have so far found only its arms and clawed hands. But these are bigger than a grown man, so the dinosaur may have been enormous!

Carnotaurus   Dilophosaurus   Ceratosaurus

- The three dinosaurs on the left were closely related to Tyrannosaurus, but none of them was as big.

Which dinosaur attacked with switchblades?

Deinonychus was a fast and deadly killer. It had sharp teeth for biting, and strong clawed hands for gripping and tearing. But its most terrible weapons were one long curved claw on each foot. When Deinonychus kicked out, its slashing claw sprang forward like a switchblade knife.

● The word Deinonychus means "terrible claw."

● Velociraptor was very similar to Deinonychus. Its name means "fast thief."

● Deinonychus probably hunted in packs to attack dinosaurs much larger than itself. African hunting dogs do this today, chasing their prey until it gets tired and slows down, then closing in for the kill.

Why did Iguanodon stick its thumbs up?

Iguanodon was a huge and gentle plant-eater, but its thumb claws were shaped like daggers. It may have used these spikes as secret weapons, stabbing with them when attacked.

Which dinosaur went fishing?

● Baryonyx was nearly built into a brick wall. The dinosaur's bones were found in a pit from which clay was being dug to make bricks.

Baryonyx had even bigger claws than Deinonychus, but it was far too large and heavy to jump up on one foot and use them as weapons. Instead, Baryonyx may have used its claws to hook fish out of rivers, just as grizzly bears do today.

Which was the biggest dinosaur?

Brachiosaurus
40 feet (12 m) high
75 feet (22.5 m) long
45 tons

Brachiosaurus was gigantic. If it were alive today, it would be able to peer over the top of a four-story building. It was so big that you would have needed to stretch up to touch its knee. And scientists have discovered bones of a long-necked dinosaur called Seismosaurus that was even bigger!

● Although Diplodocus was one of the longest dinosaurs, its head was tiny — not much bigger than a horse's head today.

● Here's how these three dinosaur giants compare with today's heaviest land animal, the African elephant.

● The long-necked dinosaurs are called sauropods. Their necks allowed them to eat leaves in the treetops that other dinosaurs couldn't reach.

● Huge dinosaurs like Brachiosaurus may have lived to be 120 years old.

Diplodocus
85 feet (26 m) long
10 tons

Which was the smallest?

Compsognathus is the smallest dinosaur found so far — it wasn't much bigger than a chicken. It ran around on two skinny legs, hunting for small animals like lizards to eat.

Apatosaurus
70 feet (21 m) long
30 tons

Did dinosaurs lay eggs?

Yes, dinosaurs laid eggs, just as today's reptiles do. The females laid them in nests on the ground.

Dinosaur eggs were different sizes and shapes — some were nearly round, others were long and thin.

● The first dinosaur eggs were found in Mongolia in the 1920s. They belonged to Protoceratops.

● The biggest dinosaur egg found so far belonged to a long-necked dinosaur called Hypselosaurus. The egg is only five times as long as a chicken's egg.

Maiasaura and babies

● Long-necked dinosaurs took care of their young, too. When the herd was on the move, the young walked in the middle, guarded by their huge parents.

● Groups of Maiasaura nested close together, just as seabirds do today.

Which dinosaur was a good mother?

In 1978, scientists made a very exciting discovery in Montana — a complete dinosaur nesting site, with nests, eggs, and even baby dinosaurs. The dinosaurs that laid the eggs were given the name Maiasaura, which means "good mother lizard."

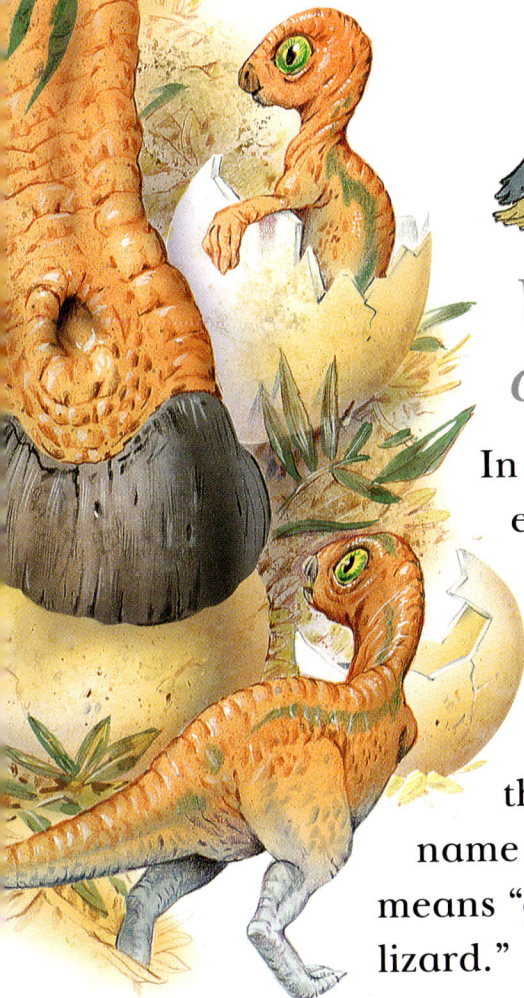

Could any dinosaurs swim?

Dinosaurs may have been able to swim if they wanted to cross a river, but they didn't live in the water. There were all kinds of other reptiles living in the oceans in dinosaur times, though — some of them even looked a little like dinosaurs.

● Some turtles were huge in dinosaur times. Archelon was longer than a rowboat.

Kronosaurus

● Kronosaurus was a real big-head! Its skull was more than twice the size of Tyrannosaurus's skull.

● Mosasaurus was a giant sea lizard.

Mosasaurus

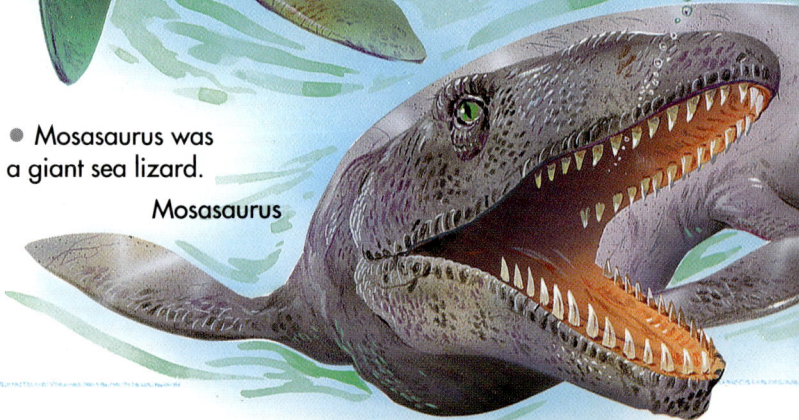

● Elasmosaurus had a long snakelike neck, similar to that of Diplodocus and the other sauropod dinosaurs. It probably swam holding its neck and tiny head out of the water, ready to lunge at passing fish.

Elasmosaurus

● These sea reptiles couldn't breathe underwater, as fish do. They had to come to the surface to breathe air, just as whales and dolphins do today.

● Ichthyosaurus looked something like a modern dolphin. It had very sharp eyes for spotting fish to eat, and it could swim very fast to catch them.

Ichthyosaurus

● The first whole skeleton of an ancient reptile ever found was that of an Ichthyosaurus. Mary and Joseph Anning were 12 and 16 years old when they discovered it at the foot of coastal cliffs in southern England in 1810.

Teleosaurus

● There were also sea crocodiles in dinosaur times. Teleosaurus's long snout was lined with lots of sharp teeth — all the better for holding on to slippery fish or squid!

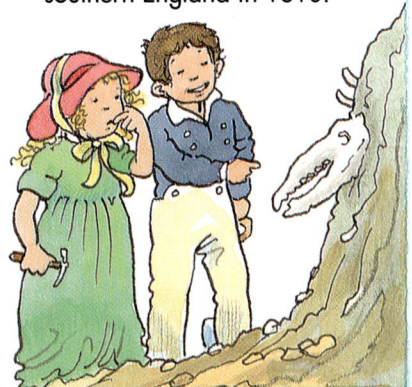

Could any dinosaurs fly?

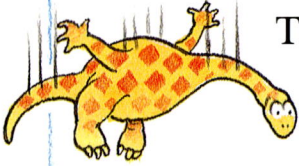

There were lots of flying reptiles in dinosaur times, but as far as we know none of them were true dinosaurs. The flying reptiles are called pterosaurs. Some were as tiny as swallows, others were huge.

● Pteranodon was bigger than any flying bird today. Its crest may have helped it to steer through the air.

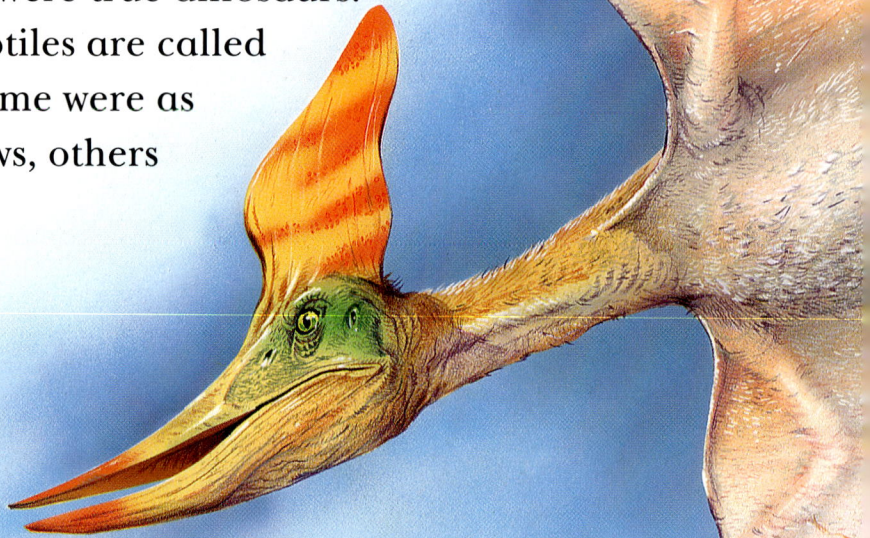

● Baby pterosaurs were probably given food by their parents in much the same way as young birds are fed today.

● The pterosaur Quetzalcoatlus was the largest flying creature the Earth has ever known. It was bigger than a modern hang-glider.

● Pterosaurs were more like bats than birds. They didn't have feathers, but most of them had soft furry bodies like bats, and leathery wings made of skin.

● Dimorphodon's head looked like a modern puffin's. Its face and mouth may have been brightly colored like a puffin's, too.

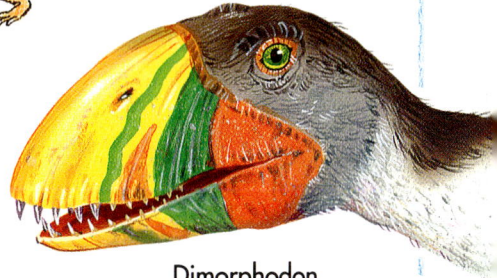

Dimorphodon

● The tip of Dzungaripterus's strange mouth would have been useful for prizing sea snails and shellfish off rocks.

Dzungaripterus

● Pterodaustro probably used its bristly bottom jaw as a strainer, to filter tiny creatures out of the water.

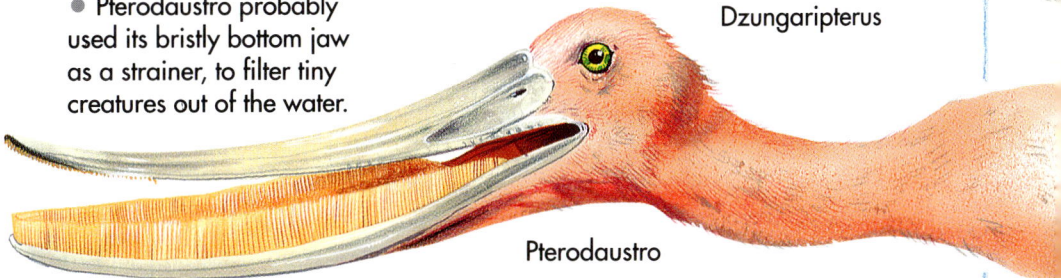

Pterodaustro

Why did Triceratops have horns?

Triceratops looked pretty fierce, but it was a plant-eater and more used to feeding than fighting. It used its three sharp horns to scare off hungry meat-eating dinosaurs — or, if that didn't work, to fight them!

● There were many different kinds of dinosaur with horns and neck frills.

● Torosaurus had the largest head of any land animal that has ever lived. With the neck frill, its head was as long as a modern car!

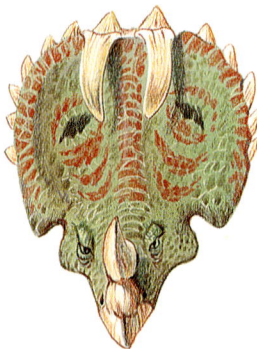

Centrosaurus

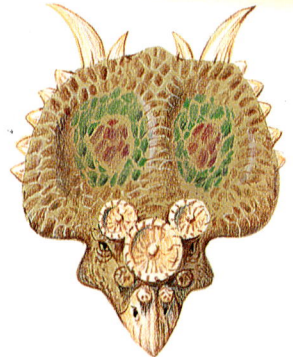

Pachyrhinosaurus

Which dinosaur had body armor?

The thick leathery skin on the top of Ankylosaurus's body had hard bony lumps and spikes growing in it. This suit of bony armor made the dinosaur into a living tank — very difficult to attack!

• Ankylosaurus may have crouched down to hide its soft belly when attacked. Meat-eaters would have broken their teeth on the armored skin over the top of its body.

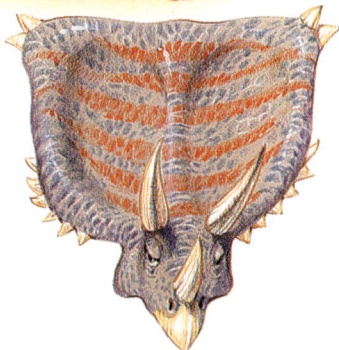

Chasmosaurus

Which dinosaur had a sting in its tail?

Stegosaurus didn't have horns — its deadly weapons were at the other end of its body. The long sharp spikes on its tail weren't poisonous like bee stingers, but they could still cause nasty wounds.

● The plates on Stegosaurus's back may have worked like solar panels, soaking up the Sun's heat and helping to keep the dinosaur warm.

● Ankylosaurus may have had eye-like patterns on its tail club. If a meat-eater thought the club was a head, it would have had a nasty surprise!

● Diplodocus's tail helped to keep it from falling over when it stretched up on its back legs to feed on high branches.

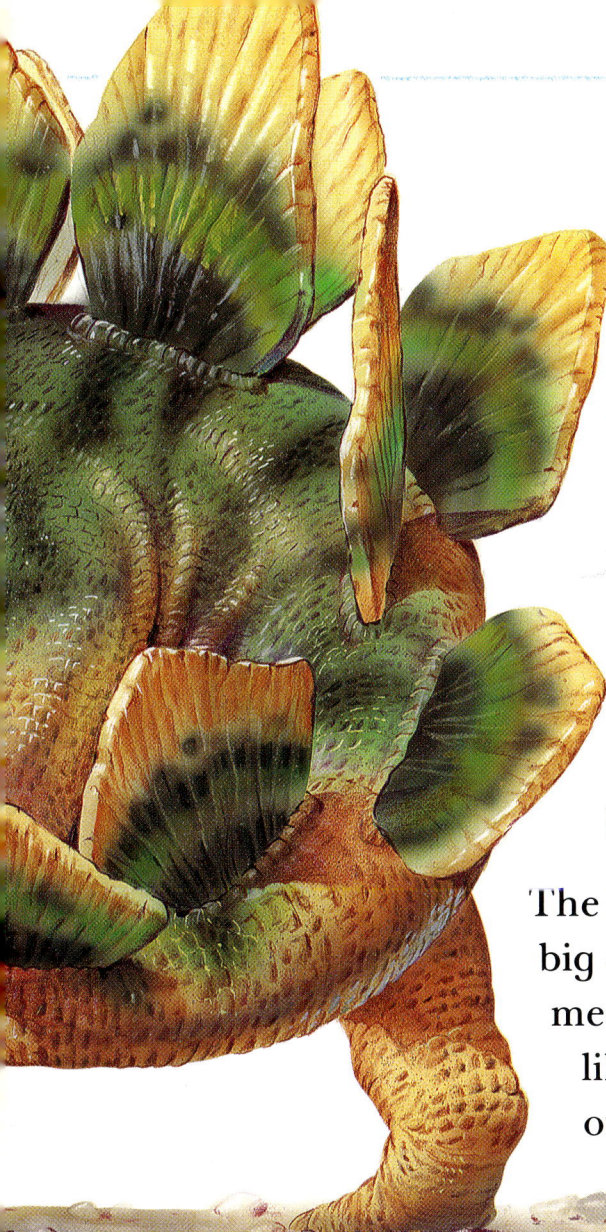

● Just as circus tightrope walkers use poles to help them balance, two-legged dinosaurs held their tails out straight for balance when running.

Which dinosaur used a whip?

The long-necked dinosaurs were big enough to scare off most meat-eaters. But if a dinosaur like Diplodocus did have to hit out at an attacker, it could lash its long tail like a whip.

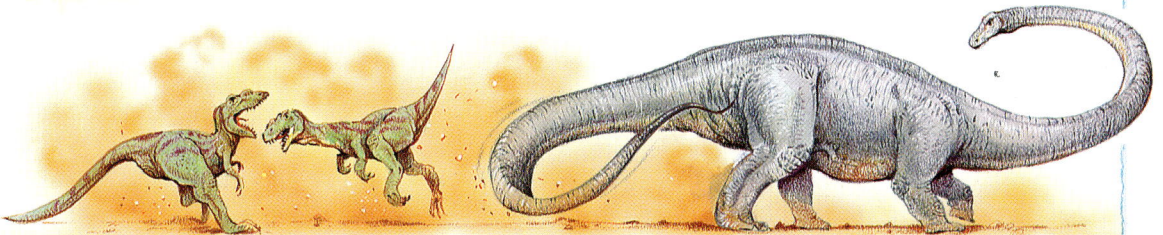

Did dinosaurs sing?

Some duck-billed dinosaurs had musical heads! Their horns and crests were hollow, like trombone pipes.

Many scientists think that by blowing through their noses, duckbills may have made a loud booming noise like a foghorn.

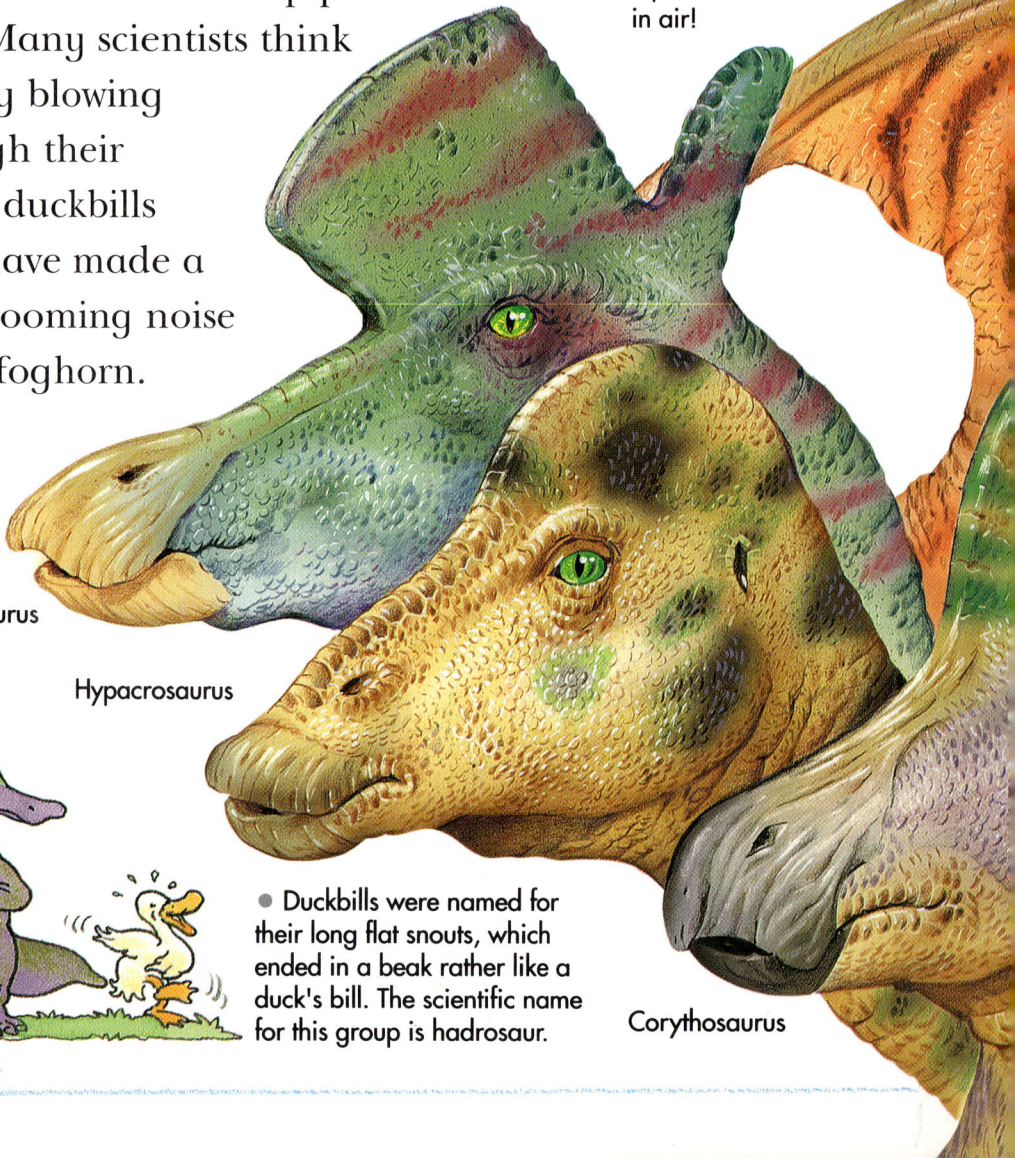

● Scientists once thought that Parasaurolophus used its long crest to breathe under water. Unfortunately, the crest didn't have holes at the top end to let in air!

Lambeosaurus

Hypacrosaurus

● Duckbills were named for their long flat snouts, which ended in a beak rather like a duck's bill. The scientific name for this group is hadrosaur.

Corythosaurus

Which dinosaurs were head-bangers?

Stegoceras had such a strong bony skull that it probably fought by headbutting. Its skull was like a crash helmet, protecting the soft brain inside.

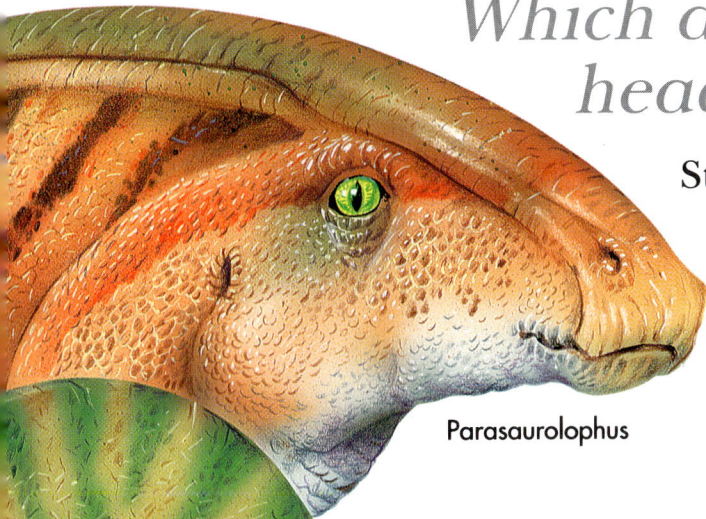

Parasaurolophus

Were dinosaurs show-offs?

Many animals like to show off to one another, particularly when trying to attract a mate. It's quite likely that some dinosaurs did, too. The duckbills may have shown off by having brightly colored and patterned crests.

● Some people think Anatosaurus might have shown off by blowing its forehead up like a balloon.

What did dinosaurs eat?

Meat-eating dinosaurs didn't just have other dinosaurs on the menu. There were lots of different creatures to eat — from insects, lizards, and birds, to small, furry, ratlike mammals. The vegetarian dinosaurs ate the leaves of plants and trees.

● As well as teeth for chewing, vegetarian dinosaurs like Psittacosaurus had horny beaks for biting through tough plant stems.

Which dinosaurs had hundreds of teeth?

Duckbilled dinosaurs had lots of tiny teeth in tightly packed rows. When they ground their top and bottom jaws together, their teeth worked like vegetable graters.

Why did dinosaurs eat stones?

Some dinosaurs swallowed small stones which collected in their stomachs like marbles in a bag. These gizzard stones worked a little like teeth, helping to grind down tough plant food.

● Stony fossils of dinosaur droppings, with bits of food inside them, help scientists to find out what dinosaurs ate.

Which dinosaur liked eggs for breakfast?

Oviraptor had a strong beak instead of teeth, and two sharp spikes in the roof of its mouth. It may have used these spikes to crack open other dinosaurs' eggs, so that it could suck out the food inside.

● Oviraptor means "egg thief."

How do we know what dinosaurs looked like?

Because no one has ever seen a living dinosaur, scientists have to work like detectives. Their main clues are fossil bones, which can be used to build a skeleton. Fossils are the stony remains of animals and plants that died a very long time ago.

● Putting dinosaur fossils together is a little like doing a jigsaw puzzle, and it's easy to make mistakes. When scientists first discovered Iguanodon, they thought its thumb spike went on its nose!

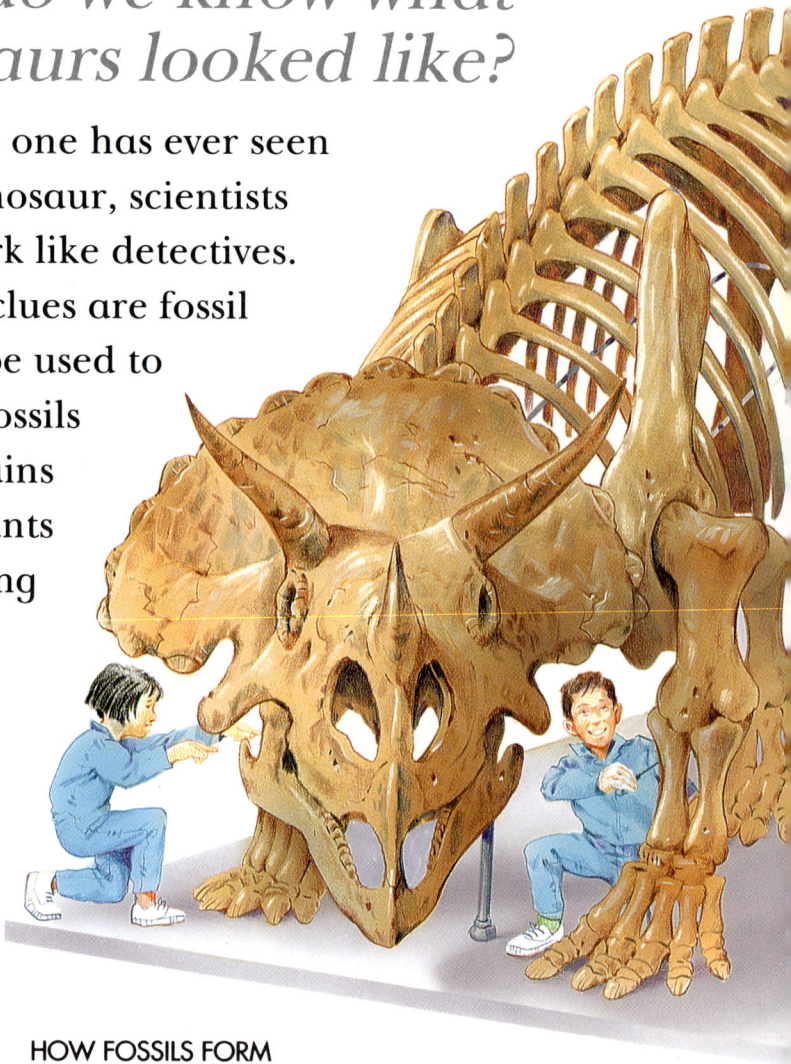

HOW FOSSILS FORM

1 A dead dinosaur was buried under a layer of sand or mud — perhaps after falling into a river or lake.

2 The soft parts of its body rotted away, leaving harder parts like the bones.

- Once they have a skeleton, scientists can work out how muscles held the bones together.

- And what the dinosaur looked like when its muscles were covered with skin.

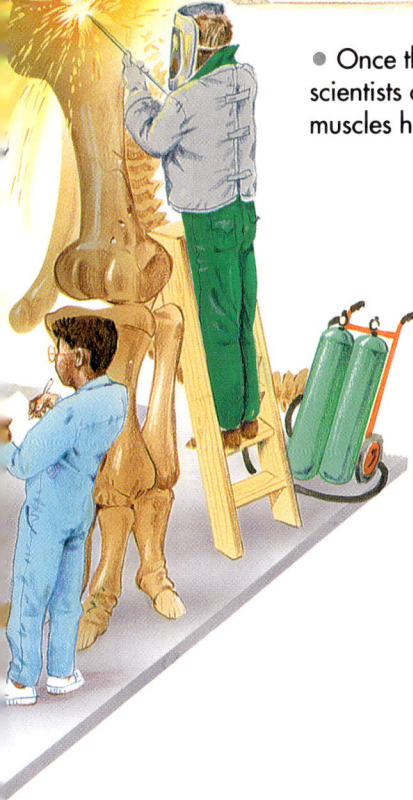

- Scientists can work out a dinosaur's weight and speed by measuring how deep its fossil footprints are, and how far they are apart.

What color were dinosaurs?

No one knows what color dinosaurs were. We have fossils of their skin, but these only show that it was scaly.

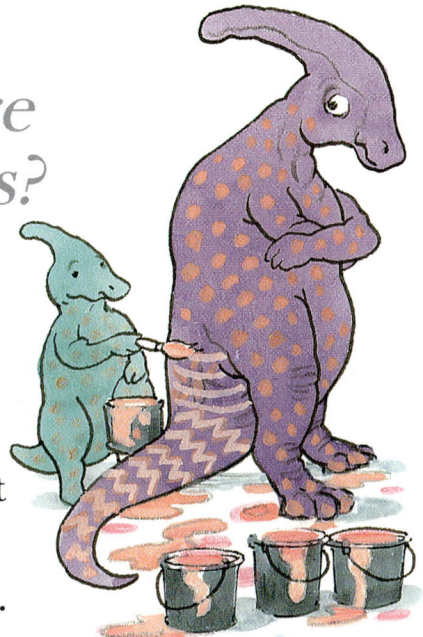

3 Over millions of years, these turned to stone.

How are dinosaur fossils found?

Dinosaur fossils are usually buried inside rock, so they have to be dug out. People sometimes stumble across them by accident, but most fossils are found by scientists who go looking in likely places. This is easier than it sounds, because only some kinds of rock have dinosaur fossils in them.

● One of the first jobs is to make a map of the digging area. Then, each time a fossil is found, it can be marked on the map.

● Fossils are usually found in sandstone, clay, limestone, or shale rocks.

● It may take weeks, months, or even years to dig out a whole skeleton.

● Dinosaurs are sometimes named after the person who found them.

● Photographs show exactly how a piece of bone was lying. This can help the scientists when they put the skeleton together again.

• The finds often have to be carried away by truck over rough bumpy ground.

• Covering a fossil in a thick layer of hard plaster helps to keep it safe from knocks. It's just like putting a plaster cast around a broken leg.

• Dinosaur digs are often in wild places, far from any town or road. The team have to live in tents or trailers.

Where are dinosaurs found?

Dinosaurs lived all over the Earth. Their fossils have been found in places as far apart as the United States and China, England and Australia, even in Antarctica!

What happened to the dinosaurs?

Something very strange happened 65 million years ago. All the dinosaurs vanished, together with all the flying reptiles and most of the sea reptiles. No one knows for sure what happened to them.

● Many scientists think giant rocks from outer space smashed into the Earth, throwing up great clouds of dust which blotted out the Sun. This changed the weather and killed off most plants. First the plant-eating dinosaurs died of cold and hunger, then the meat-eaters.

● Perhaps the dinosaurs were poisoned by new kinds of plants.

● A few people believe that sea reptiles like Elasmosaurus didn't die out, and that families of them now live in big lakes like Scotland's Loch Ness!

● Archaeopteryx looked like a dinosaur with feathers, but it wasn't. It lived 140 million years ago, and it is the oldest bird we know about. It was a very strange bird, though, because it had a tail, clawed fingers and teeth, just like a dinosaur.

Are there any dinosaurs around today?

Although there aren't any true dinosaurs alive today, we do have some of their relatives. Scientists think that birds developed from dinosaurs, because their skeletons are so similar. So look carefully the next time you see a bird nesting in a tree or hopping across the grass!

Index